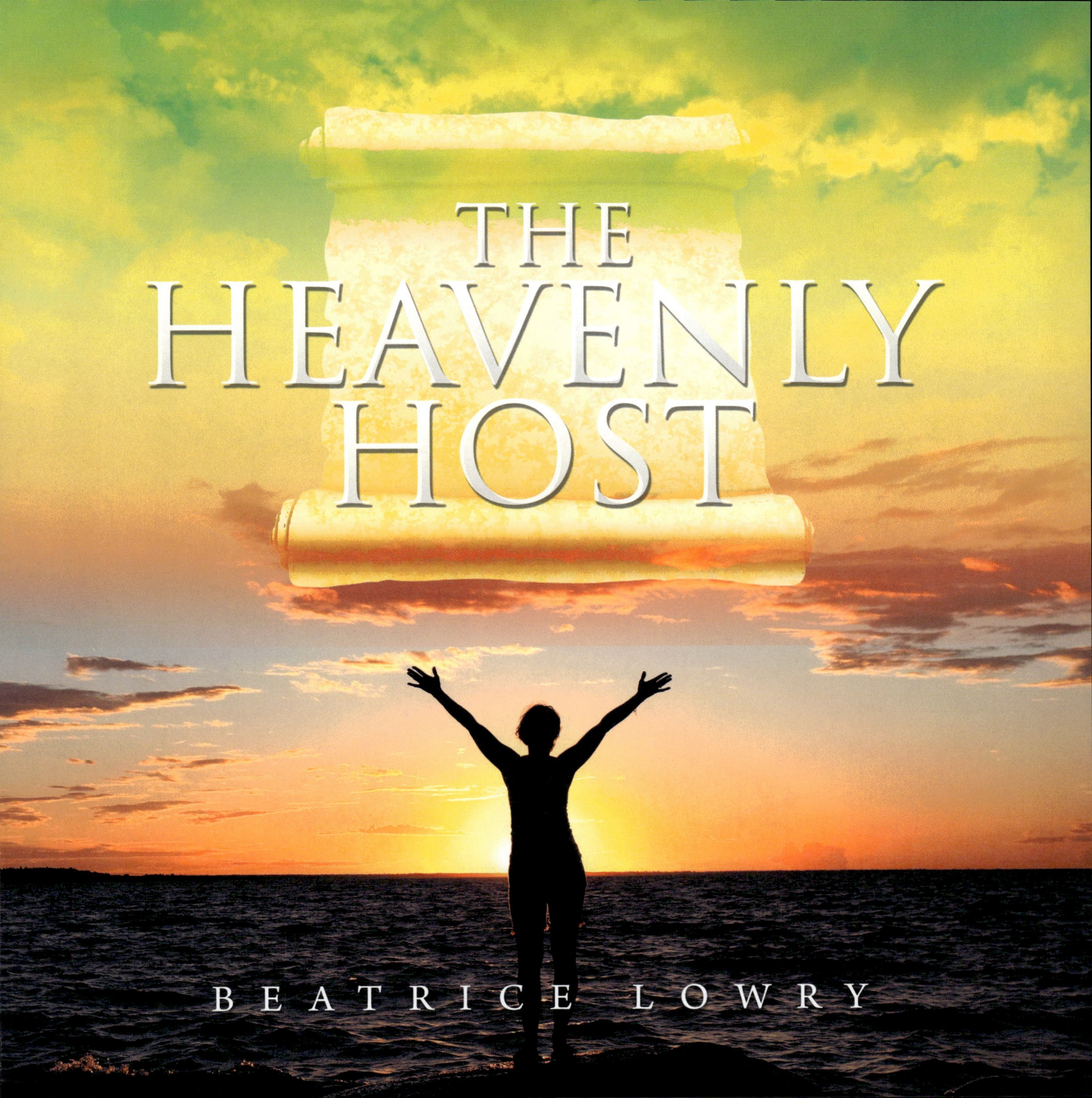
THE HEAVENLY HOST
BEATRICE LOWRY

KJV
Scripture quotations marked KJV are from the Holy Bible, King James Version (Authorized Version). First published
in 1611. Quoted from the KJV Classic Reference Bible, Copyright © 1983 by The Zondervan Corporation.

NIV
Scripture quotations marked NIV are taken from the Holy Bible, New International Version®. NIV®. Copyright © 1973,
1978, 1984 by International Bible Society. Used by permission of Zondervan. All rights reserved. [Biblica]

AuthorHouse™
1663 Liberty Drive
Bloomington, IN 47403
www.authorhouse.com
Phone: 1 (800) 839-8640

Because of the dynamic nature of the Internet, any web addresses or links contained in this book may have changed
since publication and may no longer be valid. The views expressed in this work are solely those of the author and do not
necessarily reflect the views of the publisher, and the publisher hereby disclaims any responsibility for them.

Any people depicted in stock imagery provided by Getty Images are models,
and such images are being used for illustrative purposes only.
Certain stock imagery © Getty Images.

This book is printed on acid-free paper.

ISBN: 978-1-7283-4808-7 (sc)
ISBN: 978-1-7283-4807-0 (e)

Library of Congress Control Number: 2020903796

Print information available on the last page.

Published by AuthorHouse 04/06/2020

authorHOUSE®

ACKNOWLEDGEMENTS

With Love

Giving honor to our Lord and Savior Jesus Christ. Thank God for trusting me with the "Heavenly Host".

Sending love to all my siblings in heaven and on earth; Bubba, Lonzo, Pep and LeeLee. Thank God for all family who have prayed and helped me on my journey. To my parents Elton Taylor, Sr., and Liberty Isadora Taylor.

To my mothers of the church for praying me through Mother Taylor, Mother Putney and all my church brothers and sisters.

And most of all Jesus who opened two big doors when I needed them, Apostle Timothy and Priscilla Penn and publisher Apostle Trena D. Stephenson.

Also, I would like to thank the Maggie Lena Walker Class of 1965, the greatest class ever for supporting me throughout my endeavors.

Many thanks to all thank you thank you.

Love,
Chief Prophetess Beatrice Lowry
Chief Prophetess Beatrice Lowry

FOREWORD

My first thought when I met Prophetess Bea Lowry was "this woman is incredibly serious about her walk with the Lord!" I appreciate the fact that she is serious about being an example of -what a God-fearing woman should be like. You can trust the God in her for she will say only what He tells her to say as well as do only what He tells her to do. When Bea says "Amen", she means that's ALL He said, nothing less and nothing more. She is an instrument of God's pure love who studies her gift. I have never met a more ac- curate prophet. More importantly, I can vouch for who she is – a bona fide child of God.

It is impossible for me to write an unbiased foreword. I simply love the God in this woman! In The Heavenly Host Prophet Bea encourages us to pay attention to Church Order. 1 Corinthians 12:27-31 (KJV):

27 Now ye are the body of Christ, and members in particular.

28 And God hath set some in the church, first apostles, secondarily prophets, thirdly teachers, after that miracles, then gifts of healings, helps, governments, diversities of tongues.

29 Are all apostles? are all prophets? are all teachers? are all workers of miracles?

[30] Have all the gifts of healing? do all speak with tongues? do all interpret?

[31] But covet earnestly the best gifts: and yet shew I unto you a more excellent way.

It is more important than ever before that those of us who are deliberately maturing in Him to lead by example. Cer- tainly we know that we cannot lead if we have not followed! And, if we choose not to follow the Order of God, we truly WILL NOT follow the order or the authority of those the Lord has placed us under in the local church.

In addition to, the "Church Order", there is the "Altar Call." This woman of God, I am sure, paid a dear price in order to convey to us the importance of the call to the Altar. We cannot continue to come to the Altar without INTEND- ING to do the right thing when we leave the Altar. In other words, the altar of our hearts must be transformed before we have the power to demonstrate change in our lives.

Each chapter is scripture-based and straightforward. She tells us what we need to do, in order to, behave as a child of God. If you are serious about hearing and obeying the voice of God; then read each chapter with an open ear and heart to hear what the Spirit is saying to The Church.

Dr. Priscilla H. Penn
OWRAH Fellowship Ministries
Warrenton, VA
www.owrah.com

TABLE OF CONTENTS

CHAPTER 1

Altar Call

Isaiah 45:16-20: All the makers of idols will be put to shame and disgraced; they will go off into disgrace together. But Israel will be saved by the Lord with an everlasting salvation; you will never be put to shame or disgraced, to ages everlasting. For this is what the LORD says: "he who created the heavens, he is God; he who fashioned and made the earth, he founded it; he did not create it to be empty, but formed it to be inhabited" – he says: "I am the LORD, and there is no other. I have not spoken in secret, from somewhere in a land of darkness; I have not said to Jacob's descendants, 'Seek me in vain.' I, the LORD, speak the truth; I declare what is right." "Gather together and come; assemble, you fugitives from the nations. Ignorant are those who carry about idols of wood, who pray to gods that cannot save." (NIV)

Revelation 4:8: Each of the four living creatures had six wings and was covered with eyes all around, even under his wings. Day and night they never stop saying: "Holy, holy, holy is the Lord God Almighty. Who was, and is, and is to come." – Amen (NIV)

When altar call is taking place on earth in our so- called man-made altar, some walk down like they are going to a fashion show, others walk like "let me go act like I am saved by the Lord." And then, there are those who have fornicated and have been going to the altar all their years, and they are still going and have not been delivered from their "flesh". While others are still whoring after their idols and false gods; it has become tradition just to go and kneel at the altar. There are those at the altar saying in their hearts, wishing church will please let out so they can get a cold beer, Jack Daniels, Brandy, snort, sniff, shoot needles in their arms, their penis, and vaginas, meanwhile we had 'Altar Call'. "STOP IN THE NAME OF JESUS. BEFORE YOU DROP DEAD, DON'T PLAY ON THE HOLY ALTAR."

1 Peter 2:11-12: Dear friends, I urge you, as aliens and strangers in the world, to abstain from sinful desires, which way against your soul. Live such good lives among the pagans that, though they accuse you of doing wrong, they may see your good deeds and glorify God on the day he visits us. (NIV)

Acts 5:1-12: Now a man named Ananias, together with his wife Sapphira, also sold a piece of property. With his wife's full Knowledge he kept back part of the money for himself, but brought the rest and put it at the apostles' feet. Then Peter said, "Ananias, how is it that satan has so filled your heart that you have lied to the Holy

Ghost (Spirit) and have kept for yourself some of the money you received for the land? Didn't it belong to you before it was sold? And after it was sold, wasn't the money at your disposal? What made you think of doing such a thing: You have not lied to men but to God." When Ananias heard this, he fell down and died. And great fear seized all who heard what had happened. Then the young men came forward, wrapped up his body, and carried him out and buried him. About three hours later his wife came in, not knowing what had happened. Peter asked her, "Tell me, is this the price you and Ananias got for the land?" "Yes," she said, "that is the price." Peter said to her, "How could you agree to test the Spirit of the Lord? Look! The feet of the men who buried your husband are at the door, and they will carry you out also" – Amen. At that moment, she fell down at his feet and died. Then, the young men came in and, finding her dead, carried her out and buried her beside her husband. Great fear seized the whole church and all who heard about these events. The apostles performed many miraculous signs and wonders among the people.

This is what needs to take place on earth in the church on the altar today. We need the Spirit of the Lord Christ Jesus to fall on the altar with fire to consume our 'idols', and 'false gods'.

Exodus 28:36: And thou shall make a plate of pure gold, and grave upon it like the engravings of signet, "HOLINESS TO THE LORD."

The altar on earth as you enter into the door of the church there should be a sign engraved 'Tabernacle'. Which is the holy place of God's presence among his people.

Exodus 39:30: They made the plate, the sacred diadem (crown), out of pure gold and engraved on it, like an inscription on a seal: HOLY TO THE LORD. (NIV)

The crown signified the distinction assigned to the priest, who is Jesus Christ, as one being HOLY TO THE LORD. Zechariah 14:20: On that day HOLY TO THE LORD will be inscribed on the bells of the horses, and the cooking pots in the LORD's house will be like the sacred bowls in front of the altar. (NIV)

At the altar nothing is finished until the body of Christ does what God has commanded to his people.

1 Peter 1:15-16: But just as he who called you is holy, so be holy in all you do; for it is written; "Be holy, because I am holy."

1 Peter 2:9-10: But you are a chosen people, a royal priesthood, a holy nation, a people belonging to God, that you may declare the praises of him who called you out of darkness into his wonderful light. Once you were not a people, but now you are the people of God; once you had not received mercy, but now you have received mercy.

Until, the people of God become one and of one accord as the Son and the Father, and in one place, the people of God will not see "signs and wonders."

Acts 2:1: When the day of Pentecost came, they were all together in one place. (NIV emphasis added.)

Revelation 4:8: Each of the four living creatures had six wings and was covered with eyes all around, even under his wings and was covered with eyes all around, even under his wings.

Day and night they never stop saying; "Holy, holy, holy is the Lord God almighty, who was, and is, and is to come." – Amen (NIV)

The Heavenly Host sees us East, West, South, North, North West, South East, North East, and South West. The Heavenly Host is lifted up looking down at us, and in heaven they (Fourbeast) are saying Holy, Holy, Holy, which means the Lord lifted High. People are at the altar crying give me, give me, give me. Not the Holy Spirit they are crying for, but things. No true repentance going on in their hearts. Lusting after flesh, wishing what you had last night (Baal). Your tongues are cursing the altar of the Lord. And even your thoughts are wicked in your mind in the presence of God, which is unholy in the sight of God. – Romans 1:18-23 (NIV)

Sodom and Gomorrah at the Altar.

Genesis 19: 1-29

Syphilis is a disease in the blood. Left unchecked will cause blindness, debilitation in the legs, and deterioration in the brain, leaving you helpless. And Gonorrhea leaves you with painful discharges and left unchecked will cause great agony.

This is what will happen in men. Now, for women there are often no symptoms because men are the projectors and women receivers.

But we are shouting and going to Heaven, and none have truly been born again according to St. John 3:3, 5. In reply Jesus declared, "I tell you the truth, no one can see the kingdom of God unless he is born again." Jesus answered, "I tell you truth, no one can enter the kingdom of God unless he is born of water and the Spirit.

If we really understood worship at the altar, we all would kneel and bow your heads, and stand in awe, and in fear (knowledge) of the Holy One of Israel.

Come Lord Jesus – Revelations 22:20 – Amen

Isaiah 45:21-23: Declare what is to be, present it – let them take counsel together. Who foretold this long ago, who declared it from the distant past? Was it not I, the LORD? And there is no God apart from me, a righteous God and a Savior; there is none but me. "Turn to me and be saved, all you ends of the earth; for I am God, and there is no other. By myself I have sworn, my mouth has uttered in all integrity a word that will not be revoked; Before me every knee will bow; by me every tongue will swear (confess). (NIV emphasis added)

Revelation to the church the so-called Disciples of Christ, the Holy Ones of Israel according to Isaiah 45:23. For you who say I will not bow, or to you who say it does not take all that, you will, and shall not confess that to a Holy, Holy, Holy man who looks like a Jasper stone; and angels all around standing more than 9 feet tall. You will be like a person drowning in water that does not know how to swim.

– Amen

Revelation 4:3: … A rainbow, resembling and emerald, encircled the throne. (NIV)

Revelation 22:1: Then the angel showed me the river of the water of life, as clear as crystal, flowing from the throne of God and of the Lamb. (NIV)

Worship leads to Glory, repentance leads to acceptance that He is Christ, the anointed, and Jesus is the Son of God as written in St. John 3:16. God, the Son and us.

Matthew 3:16-17: As soon as Jesus was baptized, he went up out of the water. At that moment heaven was opened, and he saw the Spirit of God descending like a dove and lighting on him. And a voice from heaven said, "This is my Son, whom I love; with him I am well please."

You must realize that you can't give Jesus anything like Cain. Genesis 4:5-6.

Come Lord Jesus – Amen

Psalm 7:9: O righteous God, who searches minds and hearts, bring to an end the violence of the wicked and make the righteous secure. (NIV)

Jeremiah 39:33: This is the covenant I will make with the house of Israel after that time," declares the Lord. "I will put my law in their minds and write it on their hearts. I will be their God, and they will be my people. (NIV)

Ephesians 4:23: to be made new in the attitude of your minds; (NIV)

Colossians 3:2: Set your minds on things above, not on earthly things. (NIV)

Dying from self and falling dead at his feet and get up with a renewed mind, and a new heart. Acts 9:23 (NIV). How? Pray until you see him, pray until you hear him, pray until you respect him and stand in awe of His Holy power on you like the day of Pentecost. Acts 2:1-4 - Amen.

When you leave the altar you should have a new tongue, not to speak things of the flesh. Galatians 5:16-26. (KJV) In other words when we are at the altar, we should be eating the rolls or roll (The Holy Word). Revelation 1:17 and Revelation 1:10.

We have not fallen in love with Jesus Christ, we think in our own human mind we have. Love is truly dying and leaving this old body and be born again from Cain's spirit and receiving Jesus' spirit until you see only the Son of God. Revelation 5:9.

Come Lord Jesus – Amen

CHAPTER 2

Leprosy In The Body of Christ

Isaiah 61:10: I delight greatly in the Lord; my soul rejoices in my God. For he has clothed me with garments of salvation and arrayed me in a robe of righteousness, as a bridegroom adorns his head like a priest and as a bride adorns herself with her jewels. (NIV)

The Hebrew word Sara' at and the Greek word lepra are both translated "Leprosy" in older versions, a wide variety of diseases that causes sores or eruptions on the skin. The Body of Christ, the "Anointed ones", the disciples, the children of God, the bold and not so beautiful are being called "infectious", the Body of Christ has "skin diseases" and "The Heavenly Host" is watching you, your children, your children's children "oozing" from your unclean lips and lifestyles.

Some of you are saying, as you read these words, "oozing?" Yes, you are oozing. AIDS, Herpes, HIV, Oral Sores, and Chlamydia. We are "shouting", "singing", "praying", and going on to heaven. NOT SO!!! "Stop!" "The Heavenly Host" are watching you. Psalm 33:18-19.

"The Heavenly Host" says some of you can't win souls or the young or the sinner, because when they looked on you they see one eye, one leg, one hand, no nose, no feet, one foot, no toe, no neck, no mouth, you are looking "retarded" with a form of godliness. Retard: to make slow; delay the development or progress of (an action, process, etc.); hinder or impede.

1 Corinthians 3:2: I gave you milk, not solid food, for you were not yet ready for it. Indeed, you are still not ready. (NIV)

2 Timothy 3:5: having a form of godliness but denying its power. Have nothing to do with them. (NIV)

Darkness looking inside the church and see sin and sickness and they say "I don't want that, I have enough health problems." They see people defeated and not victorious. They see unclean, and not clean. They see aborted babies dead and not alive. They see the fetus that has a disfigured feature and body.

2 Kings 1:16-17: He told the king, "This is what the LORD says: Is it because there is no God in Israel for you to consult that you have sent messengers to consult Baal-Zebub, the god of Ekron? Because you have done this, you will never leave the bed

you are lying on. You will certainly die!" So he died, according to the word of the LORD that Elijah had spoken.

The pastor is King Ahaziah sick and waiting to die or have already died spiritually. Everything he touches or says is a lie before "The Heavenly Host."

The pastor is bleeding with the people when they worship; they are bleeding everywhere still in their own blood. Not the blood of Jesus, but "sin."

Ezekiel 16:6: Then I passed by and saw you kicking about in your blood, and as you lay there in your blood I said to you, "Live!"

My question to the Body of Christ, will you LIVE? Or will you DIE?

The young people want to be SAVED, but they see confusion. And no one really teaching; so they can be found and loved by the people of God. They see abusive relationships with Jesus and others. The young people see pastors having sex with males/women with women. They see abused mothers being beat by their daddy's, but we the church want the young people saved. How can the young people, the unwed mother, the young man who steal, who kills, who sells drugs, who pimps, not only the young girls on the streets, but the ones in church, as well. When we don't honor "The Lord Thy God." How can we introduce the young to a body filled with sores, and we are drinking from Baal's cup of drunkenness with false god's?

"The Heavenly Host" looks down as a man who sits in jail with a two-way mirror. He doesn't realize someone can see him, but he can't see them, and God said that's how he sees us. We are looking in the mirror at ourselves, but we are not looking for God, or at God in the mirror and we should, but do we?

James 1:23: Anyone who listens to the word but does not do what it says is like a man who looks at his face in a mirror.

Come Lord Jesus – Amen

CHAPTER 3

Heavenly Host

Revelation 4:2-3: And immediately I was in the spirit: and, behold, a throne was set in heaven, and one sat on the throne. And he that sat was to look upon like a jasper and a sardine stone: and there was a rainbow round about the throne, in sight like unto an emerald.

"The Heavenly Host is over the church, what we called the body of Christ, but it is not cooperating with the head, who is and always will be "The Lord of LORDS, and King of KINGS who sat and reign and looks like a jasper stone full of colors and looking down on us."

Proverbs 1:22: "How long will you simple one [The Hebrew word rendered simple in Proverbs generally denotes one without moral direction and inclined to evil].

Love your simple ways? How long will mockers delight in mockery and fools hate knowledge?

People are making a mockery of His body with foolish jesting and talking and full of flesh that smells in his nostrils.

Christ, the anointed, is waiting for us to start and began looking like our Father who art in Heaven, smelling like a sweet odor in his nostrils and dressing like Him.

2 Corinthians 2:15: For we are to God the aroma of Christ among those who are being saved and those who are perishing.

Full of the Spirit, power and might, not whoring and prostituting ourselves with false images and idols and false gods, "ourselves."

Come Lord Jesus – Amen

Revelation 19:1, 4
Revelation 21:11-27
Revelation 22:1-5

A city where the Heavenly Host live and where there are great walls and angels who are 9 feet tall or taller, where people are singing. There are 12 gates and no man; woman, boy or girl can enter. Heavily guarded by angels not police better than the White House more beautiful than the eye can see. Water flowing from His feet at the throne. No ordinary throne, like the king in England, but the King of KINGS throne. With real elders around the Lord of LORDS. – Amen

Trees that are silver called "The Tree of Life", fruit that we have never seen on earth to eat for healing.

The Holy City called the New Jerusalem. For the Lord God and the Heavenly Host reigneth. The Lord God "omnipotent." Jerusalem the land of Israel there are wars and rumors of wars. There's blood shedding in the streets. There are babies dying, women are wailing and men are crying at the Wailing Wall. She's as a woman travailing in birth, so much pain, and so much heartache. When will Israel cry out for the New Jerusalem? When will they say, "Come Lord Jesus, save us?!" Until then we are waiting for the New Jerusalem to descend from heaven with the Heavenly Host and the Lamb of God, and the great angels, Michael and Gabriel. The New Jerusalem is to be adorned as the new bride of Christ. Where King Jesus shall take his rightful place on King David's throne. – Amen

Revelation 22:17: And the Spirit and the bride say, Come. And let him that heareth say, Come. And let him that is athirst come. And whosoever will, let him take the water of life freely.

-Speak Lord Jesus Speak –

CHAPTER 4

The Gate Keeper

Genesis 28:17: And he was afraid, and said, How dreadful is this place! This is none other but the house of God, and this is the gate of heaven.

Jeremiah 17:19: Thus said the LORD unto me; Go and stand in the gate of the children of the people, whereby the kings of Judah come in, and by the which they go out, and in all the gates of Jerusalem;

Who are the Gatekeepers in heaven and earth?

Heaven: The Gatekeeper will be the angels who are at the entrance of the gate now. There are 12 angels at each gate.

Revelation 21:12: And had a wall great and high, and had twelve gates, and at the gates twelve angels, and names written thereon, which are the names of the twelve tribes of the children of Israel:

Genesis 3:24: So he drove out the man (Adam); and he placed at the east of the garden of Eden Cherubims, and a flaming sword which turned every way, to keep the way of the tree of life.

Psalm 118:20: This gate of the LORD, into which the righteous shall enter.

[*The Narrow and Wide Gates*] "Enter through the narrow gate. For wide is the gate and broad is the road that leads to destruction, and many enter through it. – Matthew 7:13

Come Lord Jesus – Amen

CHAPTER 5

The Prophet

2 Peter 3:1-10: This second epistle, beloved, I now write unto you; in both which I stir up your pure minds by way of remembrance: That ye may be mindful of the words which were spoken before by the holy prophets, and of the commandment of us the apostles of the Lord and Saviour: Knowing this first, that there shall come in the last days scoffers, walking after their own lusts, And saying, Where is the promise of his coming: For since the fathers fell asleep, all things continue as they were from the beginning of the creation. For this they willingly are ignorant of, that by the word of God the heavens were of old, and the earth standing out of the water and in the water, perished: But the heavens and the earth, which are now, by the same word are kept in store, reserved unto fire against the day of judgment and perdition of ungodly men. But, beloved, be not ignorant of this one thing, that one day is with the Lord as a thousand years, and a thousand years as one day. The Lord is not slack concerning his promise, as some men count slackness; but is longsuffering to us-ward, not willing that any should perish, but that all should come to repentance. But the day of the Lord will come as a thief in the night; in the which the heavens shall pass away with a great noise, and the elements shall melt with fervent heat, the earth and the works that are therein shall be burned up.

A prophet is a gift that God has used from the beginning of time and will use continually to the end. If you read your bible carefully with God's understanding; God always sent the prophet first, or the people were sent to the prophet and there was always a word from the Lord.

The Word of the Lord could have consisted of warning, judgment, sickness, healing, death, life, and birth. And then there were times when God told the prophets to anoint with oil for ordination. They were the mouthpieces of the Lord. Whatever God wanted to say, the prophet was able to hear and see God first. Sometimes the prophet smelled Him through the fire, smoke, water, and wind. Then there were times the Lord sent them visions and dreams to tell His people what "Thus sayeth the Lord". A seer can be a prophet. A prophet is set apart from others and peculiar like John the Baptist, one who is crying in the wilderness. A prophet doesn't compromise or sell the gift for money, clothes, jewelry, sex, filthy lucre, fornication, and no works of the flesh. The prophet should have clarity and come in the volume of the book. (The Holy Bible)

-Come Lord Jesus – Amen

A true prophet would be one who is "massa" used to indicate message of judgment.

The other word is "oracle" both are Hebrew words.

This is used 375 times in the OT, and only in divine speech.

In older versions "thus saith the Lord."

For the body of Christ today, the prophet or prophets are saying money, house, car, or things to make the peoples ears itch or want them to be liked by them. So they may receive money from the people. The people are not receiving truth, no light, all darkness and lies like the father of lies.

2 Timothy 4:3: For the time will come when they will not endure sound doctrine; but after their own lusts shall they heap to themselves teachers, having itching ears;

St John 8:44: Ye are of your father the devil, and the lusts of your father ye will do. He was a murderer from the beginning, and abode not in the truth, because there is no truth in him. When he speaketh a lie, he speaketh of his own: for he is a liar, and the father of it.

2 Timothy 2:3-4: Thou there endure hardness, as a good soldier of Jesus Christ. No man that warreth entangleth himself with the affairs of this life; that he may please him who hath chosen him to be a soldier.

And this is for the generation that may not understand what warreth means. Endure hardship with us like a good soldier of Christ Jesus. No one serving as a soldier gets involved in civilian affairs – he wants to please his commanding officer. (NIV)

Who is your commanding officer? King of KINGS, Lord of LORDS, Jesus Christ. Not the natural man. - Amen

The prophet God calls to say "thus saith the lord" has a two edged sword (tongue) like his Father and with "fire" not "water". The prophet God has does not please man, but God.

James 3:6: And the tongue is a fire, a world of iniquity: so is the tongue among our members, that it defileth the whole body, and setteth on fire the course of nature; and it is set on fire of hell.

So, when the body of Christ sees a prophet or prophetess, although Ephesians 4:11 says "Prophet": And he gave some, apostles; and some prophets; and some, evangelists; and some, pastors and teachers, they should say as the messengers of King Ahaziah said according to 2 Kings 1:7-8: And he said unto them, What manner of man was he which came up to meet you, and told you these words?

And they answered him, He was a hairy man, and girt with a girdle of leather about his loins. And he said, It is Elijah the Tishbite. It should be the same way when we stand in the church of Christ, that when the prophet walks in they shouldn't have to announce who they are, instead we should know who they are by their fruit.

John 15:5: This is to my Father's glory, that you bear much fruit, showing yourselves to be my disciples.

Ephesians 5:9: (For the fruit of the Spirit is in all goodness and righteousness and truth;)

Revelation 1:16: And he had in his right hand seven stars: and out of his mouth went a sharp twoedged sword: and his countenance was as the sun shineth in his strength.

-Come Lord Jesus – Amen

CHAPTER 6

Elijah and Elisha

2 Kings 2:4: Then Elijah said to him, "Stay here, Elisha; the LORD has sent me to Jericho." And he replied, "As surely as the LORD lives and as you live, I will not leave you." So they went to Jericho. (NIV)

This is an example of the elderly men training the young men of this generation today. 1 Timothy 5:1-2: Rebuke not an elder, but intreat him as a father; and the younger men as brethren; the elder women as mothers; the younger as sisters, with all purity. As for the younger women today, what man calls "prophetess", they should be trained like Naomi and Ruth. Ruth 1:11, 16: And Naomi said, Turn again, my daughters: why will ye go with me: Are there yet any more sons in my womb, that they may be your husbands? And Ruth said, Intreat me not to leave thee, or to return from following after thee: for whither thou goest, I will go; and where thou lodgest, I will lodge: thy people shall be my people, and thy God my God:

We are not training prophets according to God's word. Where are the Elisha's that need to stand with the Elijah's? Where are the Ruth's that needs to stand with the Naomi's?

2 Kings 2:6: And Elijah said unto him, Tarry, I pray thee, here; for the LORD had sent me to Jordan. And he said, As the LORD liveth, and as thy soul liveth, I will not leave thee. And they two went on.

Where are the Elisha's that want the double portions? Where are the Ruth's that want the double portions? No matter what happens in life with them, the Heaven Host needs you wants you.

Matthew 18:19: Again I say unto you, That if two of you shall agree on earth as touching any thing that they shall ask, it shall be done for them of my Father which is in heaven.

When will you come?

When will you answer the call?

When will you say yes, to be in agreement with the Heavenly Host?

When will you say yes, to have your name on the Heavenly Host roll? When? Some of you are saying 'have my name on the roll? Or have my name in the book'? Yes the book! Yes the book! Yes the book! Yes the book!

Revelation 3:5: He that overcometh, the same shall be clothed in white raiment; and I will not blot out his name out of the book of life, but I will confess his name before my Father, and before his angels.

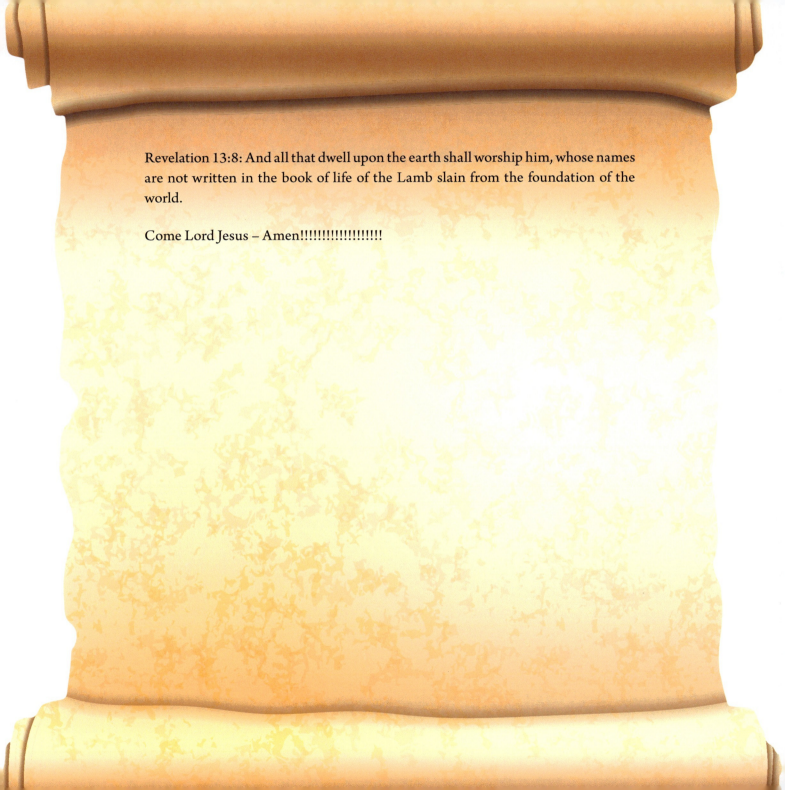

Revelation 13:8: And all that dwell upon the earth shall worship him, whose names are not written in the book of life of the Lamb slain from the foundation of the world.

Come Lord Jesus – Amen!!!!!!!!!!!!!!!!!!!

CHAPTER 7

The Church Order On Earth

1 Corinthians 12:27-31

But man has turned the order of the body of Christ into a mockery. There will be and always have been a prophet to every congregation to be a seer and to let the pastor of the church and the congregation know what "thus say the Lord."

God has an order for the people of God and always will. No matter what man has said or does. God Spokesperson, He uses the "Prophet" to bring reverence to the Body and to the Pastor.

The "two P's" should always work very close together in "unity." The Prophet should have freedom of the church in the true and living spirit of Jesus to walk, talk, and be able to say to the congregation, "this is of God."

"The Prophet" whether "male or female" young, or old should be able to walk on water in front of "The Heavenly Host" and "The Body of Christ."

EPHESIANS 4:4-12

FIRST APOSTLE
SECOND PROPHETS
THIRD TEACHERS
MIRACLES
GIFTS OF HEALINGS
HELPS
GOVERNMENTS
DIVERSITIES OF TONGUE
PASTORS
EVANGELISTS

CHAPTER 8

The Heavenly Congregation

The Cherubims

Ezekiel 10:3-4: Now the cherubim were standing on the right side of the temple when the man entered, and the cloud filled the inner court. Then the glory of the LORD went up from the cherub to the threshold of the temple, and the temple was filled with the cloud and the court was filled with the brightness of the glory of the LORD.

God the Father

Romans 8:15: For ye have not received the spirit of bondage again to fear; but ye have received the Spirit of adoption, whereby we cry, Abba, Father.

The Son of God, Christ Jesus

Luke 1:31-32: And, behold, thou shalt conceive in thy womb, and bring forth a son, and shalt call his name JESUS. He shall be great, and shall be called the Son of the Highest: and the Lord God shall give unto him the throne of his father David:

King of Kings, Lord of Lords

Revelation 19:16: And he hath on his vesture and on his thigh a name written, KING OF KINGS, AND LORD OF LORDS.

The Elders Around the Throne

Revelation 4:4: And round about the throne were four and twenty seats: and upon the seats I saw four and twenty elders sitting, clothed in white raiment; and they had on their heads crowns of gold.

Gabriel

Daniel 8:16, 9:12: And I heard a man's voice between the banks of Ulai, which called, and said, Gabriel, make this man to understand the vision. And he hath confirmed his words, which he spake against us, and against our judges that judged us, by bringing upon us a great evil: for under the whole heaven hath not been done as hath been done upon Jerusalem.

Michael

Daniel 10:13: But the prince of the kingdom of Persia withstood me one and twenty days: but, lo, Michael, one of the chief princes, came to help me; and I remained there with the kings of Persia.

Seraphims "The Burning Ones"

Isaiah 6:2: Above it stood the seraphims: each one had six wings; with twain he covered his face, and with twain he covered his feet, and with twain he did fly. Revelation 4:7-8: And the first beast was like a lion, and the second beast like a calf, and the third beast had a face as a man, and the fourth beast was like a flying eagle. And the four beasts had each of them six wings about him; and they were full of eyes within: and they rest not day and night, saying, Holy, holy, holy, LORD God Almighty, which was, and is, and is to come.

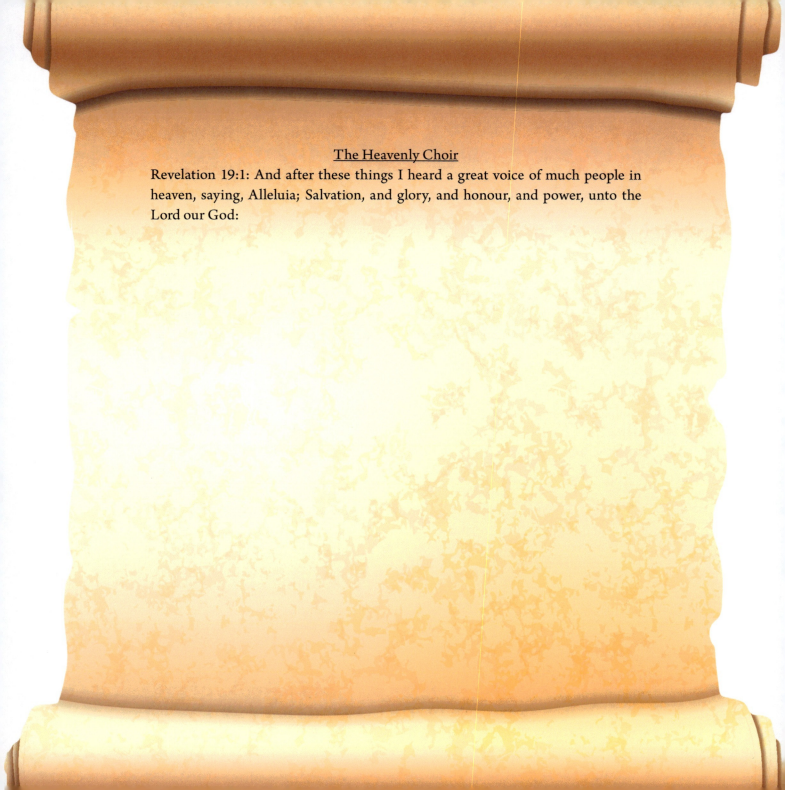

The Heavenly Choir

Revelation 19:1: And after these things I heard a great voice of much people in heaven, saying, Alleluia; Salvation, and glory, and honour, and power, unto the Lord our God:

CHAPTER 9

"Mothers' of the Church for the Body of Christ

Luke 2:36-38: And there was one Anna, a prophetess, the daughter of Phannuel, of the tribe of Aser: she was of a great age, and had lived with an husband seven years from virginity; And she was a widow of about fourscore and four (84) years, which departed not from the temple, but served God with fastings and prayers night and day. And she coming in that instant gave thanks likewise unto the Lord, and spake of him to all them that looked for redemption in Jerusalem.

Where are the mothers sitting at the entrance of the tabernacle of the church? Waiting for the entrance of Jesus to save souls. Where are the true apostolic mothers who God called from the foundation of time?

Genesis 2:22: And the rib, which the LORD God had taken from man, made him a woman, and brought her unto the man.

Genesis 3:20: And Adam called his wife's name Eve; because she was the mother of all living.

Eve is the first mother to give birth to Cain and Abel. Where is the mother Eve in the body of Christ? Then he calls on Abrahams with Sara, the second mother to give birth to Isaac in her old age 90 years. Where are the Sara's in the body of Christ? Next, Mary, the mother of Jesus; the greatest of them all (at the age of 14 years), why? Because she brought forth Messiah. So, the Bible lets us know that a true born again, spirit filled, baptized with fire, tongue speaking mother, holy and just, and undefiled from the world can become a mother at any age in the Lord Jesus Christ the Anointed.

1 Corinthians 3:16-17: Know ye not that ye are the temple of God, and that the Spirit of God dwelleth in you? If any man defile the temple of God, him shall God destroy; for the temple of God is holy, which temple ye are.

1 Corinthians 6:17-20: But he that is joined unto the Lord is one spirit. Flee fornication. Every sin that a man doeth is without the body; but he that committeth fornication sinneth against his own body. What? Know ye not that your body is the temple of the Holy Ghost which is in you, which is in you, which ye have of God, and ye are not your own? For ye are bought with a price: therefore glorify God in your body, and in your spirit, which are God's.

What is the meaning of a "Mother?"

Webster's (NW) states that a mother is female "first" not male, with a "penis", motherhood with a "womb", to produce and bring forth (Isaac's and Jacob's). And Mary the mother of Jesus was our first example for all women over the world. She brought forth "The Messiah" our Lord and Savior, the Bright and Morning star. Mothers are not "Lesbians", you can't teach daughters how to masturbate, or use their vagina with a vagina. Their bodies are not for prostitution; their mouths are for the praise of God and not the abominable things of the world. Mothers don't teach your daughters to miscarry in the spiritual womb or natural. They are to be taught how to abstain from fornication, and abstain their minds of all filthy thoughts of Jezebel.

Is the Mother a cocoon or butterfly for the cross? Has the mother, the real mother been transformed like Christ? Has her mind been renewed in the things of Jesus? Let this mind be in you like Christ Jesus "Balanced", not heavenly and no earthly good. The mother's are the first teacher to her sons and daughters. A mother sits at the entrance of the door for the Body of Christ and waits like Anna the prophet did to behold Jesus.

Old, but holy, old, but just, old; but eyes to see and wisdom to bestow on the daughters who come to the house of God.

Is the mother a cocoon (not ready) or butterfly fully matured and full of colors like Jesus?

Revelation 1:14-15: His head and his hairs were white like wool, as white as snow; and his eyes were as a flame of fire; And his feet like unto fine brass, as if they burned in a furnace; and his voice as the sound of many waters.

Mothers are butterflies with four "broad wings". Where are the mothers of Israel and the mothers of gentiles who have four wings?

'One Wing'; Agape Love
'Second Wing'; Compassion
'Third Wing'; Wisdom
'Fourth Wing'; Guidance

We need these mothers in the church for the young girls and some old girls. Where are the butterflies that God called? The Heavenly Host mothers' who have beauty about them like Jesus in heaven.

Revelation 4:3: And the one who sat there had the appearance of jasper and carnelian. A rainbow, resembling an emerald, encircled the throne.

We can't tell the real mothers from the false mothers. Who are the false mothers?

1 Kings 3:16: Then came there two women, that were harlots (prostitutes), unto the king, and stood before him.

False mothers have incest with their children; whether they are male or female. When the false mother lay on the spirit of the children in the Body of Christ and don't teach them and lead them, they die, spiritually and naturally. A false mother steals the true daughters and sons from the church, leading them astray.

Genesis 25:26: After this, his brother came out, with his hand grasping Esau's heel; so he was named Jacob. [Jacob means he grasps the heel -figuratively, he deceives]. (NIV)

1 Kings 3:19-20: During the night this woman's son died because she lay on him. So she got up in the middle of the night and took my son from my side while I your servant was asleep. She put him by her breast and put her dead son by my breast. (NIV)

A false mother cannot give milk when there is no milk in her breast to feed for the word of God. (Barren Breast) 1 Peter 2:2: As newborn babes, desire the sincere milk of the word, that ye may grow thereby: (NIV)

We can't tell the real mother from the false mothers. Mothers want to look 16 years of age instead of their real age.

Wearing long dresses to your ankles, to your feet doesn't make you a mother. No foundation on your face and no "red lips" doesn't make you a mother; no blond hair doesn't make you a mother. It has nothing to do with the outer appearance, but all to be about the transformation of looking like Jesus and being Jesus in the spirit. When you see the mother you should see Jesus, when you see Me you should see the Father.

Where are the Anna's who sit at the door of the church and wait for the sick and unlovable?

Mothers are called by God and then man. Anything God ordained has goodness, mercy, and truth about their neck and heart...

Nehemiah 9:17: And refused to obey, neither were mindful of thy wonders that thou didst among them; but hardened their necks, and in their rebellion appointed a captain to return to their bondage: but thou art a God ready to pardon, gracious and merciful, slow to anger, and of great kindness, and forsookest them not.

All good and perfect gifts come from above. Just like looking out among you to find seven holy deacons. 1 Timothy 3:8. We, (the body of Christ) should be able to look out and choose a God fearing woman or women who love Jesus, teach Jesus, and be able to lead by example and not by talking. To have agape love, true love for the daughters that come in naked, poor in spirit, abused, raped, molested (mentally and physically). Who doesn't have a real mother at home or maybe the mother has died naturally or spiritually and she needs to be resurrected from her Hagar issues and be loved and taught herself.

Genesis 16:3: And Sarai Abram's wife took Hagar her maid the Egyptian, after Abram had dwelt ten years in the land of Canaan, and gave her to her husband Abram to be his wife.

There are mothers who are like Hagar that have been used and abused, and no one has really taught them how to be healed and be real mothers, so therefore; we have a lot of Hagar issues's in the Body of Christ.

So, mothers lay yourself at the altar of the Lord and listen for his call. No matter who you are or what you have done the Lord desires to heal and mend your heart. He desires to solve your "issues" in life and make you complete. He desires to make you Beautiful inside and out just like the butterfly ever so graceful and full of colors.

Conclusion: I was once a cocoon deeply stained within. Full of shame. But Jesus took me in and now I am a Beautiful Butterfly…Full of broad wings…Full of Color. Before my mother went home to be with the Lord on November 18,

1982, I had a vision of Jesus and these beautiful colors. And she said to me, "Bea, God wants you to be as beautiful as those colors and real as those colors in Him." My mother Liberty Isadora Bostick Taylor prophesied these words to me. Peace!!!!!!!!

-Come Lord Jesus – Amen

CHAPTER 10

Our Mother

Liberty Isadora Bostick born in Allendale, SC. The eleventh child of 13 children. Married Mr. Elton Taylor, Sr., from Waynes County, NC.

Out of their union five children:

(1) Beatrice Taylor, (2) Elton Taylor, Jr. (3) Alonzo Taylor Sr., (4) Alphonzo Taylor, Sr. and (5) Arthea Taylor.

Our mother and father decided to separate when I was 13 years old. Our mother didn't leave us, didn't abandon us, and didn't give us up to welfare. But being the woman she was, she asked for information and found what she needed for her five children. She fed us when she didn't eat. We all drank out of a 16 oz. Pepsi soda and I was last to drink. She said I would spit when drinking, in other words, I didn't know how to drink out of the 16 oz bottle, with my siblings and my mother.

My mother became a single mother of a house with five children, three boys, and two girls.

We had to move to the projects, but we grew and survived with her and learned from her how to be aggressive and assertive because she was the father and mother.

Our mother sent us to church every Sunday, with a Baptist deacon, who had a station wagon, who came to our front door and drove us to church, Sunday School, morning service and back home to our Mom until we learned how to walk to church, like 3 or 4 blocks all five. Number 3 child had a speech problem he was like Moses, and our Mother lay hands, when we didn't know what laying hands and praying and believing Jesus for healing and it happen with no money, Jesus made a way for speech therapy free of charge. We all had gifts from our mother's womb, football, basketball, management, nurse, leaders, hard worker and loving our mother and respecting her. But one thing for sure it wasn't easy for her only making $15.00 a week. But, thank God for the projects, which you call now RRHA. Our mother was a great woman and a great praying woman, and loved people and life. RIP: May 7, 1928 - November 18, 1982.

ABOUT THE AUTHOR

Chief Prophetess Beatrice Lowry

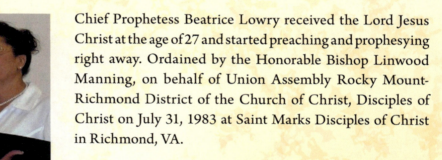

Chief Prophetess Beatrice Lowry received the Lord Jesus Christ at the age of 27 and started preaching and prophesying right away. Ordained by the Honorable Bishop Linwood Manning, on behalf of Union Assembly Rocky Mount-Richmond District of the Church of Christ, Disciples of Christ on July 31, 1983 at Saint Marks Disciples of Christ in Richmond, VA.

After laying on of the hands by the Honorable Bishop T.D. Jakes in West Virginia in April 1995, and returning to Richmond, God gave the vision of A.D.I. Ministries on a 50 day fast in July 1995 to Evangelist/Chief Prophetess Bea Lowry. Evangelism Radio Ministry started on WFTH Faith Radio Station on Saturday mornings at 7 a.m. Since, then God has called her to another gift according to Ephesians

4:11 and that is to pastor to all people. From her Pastor's vision of International in his ministry in Dallas, TX, she saw the vision and ran with it according to Habakkuk

2:3 for A.D.I. Ministries International. She also had the pleasure to sing with the crusade choir for Benny Hinn Ministries, at the Richmond Coliseum in 1999.

Besides pastoring, she is a spiritual mother of many children, Prayer Warrior, Confidant, Soloist, and also Healer for many broken hearts. As an employee at Senior Connection, The Capital Area Agency on Aging, an advocacy for the Senior Connection Choral Group, it allows ministry to the whole person – feeding the homeless, clothing the homeless and finding employment and working with ex-offenders.

As Founder/Overseer of A.D.I. Ministries, Chief Prophetess Bea Lowry has a LOVE for battered women, youth revivals and women conferences; preaching at other churches – wherever and whenever God opens the door. She went on a mission trip to Predras Negras, COAHUILA, Mexico in 2001. Chief Prophetess Bea Lowry allowed God to use her in healing, saving souls, and also feeding many children and ministering to special needs. She saw the mighty hand of God move mightily.

God sent Chief Prophetess Bea Lowry to pastor 36 people at the Wyndham Hotel in Richmond, VA. Held services every 3rd Sunday from July to December 2000. God then spoke and said "STEP OUT ON FAITH", and began Sunday School and worship services EVERY Sunday beginning January 2001 until November 2002. Bubba's Boys (named after her brother Elton Taylor, Jr.) was given September 30, 2001 at 4:00 p.m. in Chief Prophetess Bea Lowry's home, after with A.D. I. Ministries International. Dora's Girls (named after my mother Liberty Isadora

Bostick Taylor) was given after prayer at 5:00 a.m. on that morning on Chief Prophetess Bea's knees.

Chief Prophetess Lowry has the divine favor of God, which has allowed her to sit under the guidance and teaching of Bishop Tudor Bismark, who resides in Harare, Zimbabwe; who came to the United States for a KINGDOM SUMMIT, RESTORATION of the FIVE-FOLD Ministry Leaders Round-Table that was held at Stratford Hall Plantation in June 2004. Chief Prophetess Lowry loves the Lord and loves ALL people, and can't wait until Jesus returns according to 1 Thessalonians 4:15-18. Amen!

Education and Awards

Educated in the Richmond Public Schools. Graduated from Richmond Technical School of Nursing on August 23, 1984. Graduated from Virginia Union School of Theology (Evans Smith Program for Christian Education) on May 20, 1995. Attended Smithdeal Massey Business College.

Received many outstanding awards especially employee of the month from the Richmond Airport Hilton Hotel. Certificate of Appreciation from Upjohn Health Care Nursing. Certificate of Appreciation from the Baptist Convention for participation in 1997 at Triumphant Baptist Church. Recognition from Sharon Baptist Church on Abortion from the City of Richmond.

UPCOMING BOOK
RELEASE:

MOTHERS WITH 'BROAD WINGS'

Printed in the United States
By Bookmasters